Golden Years Lifestyle

Alternative Home Ownership

For Young Minded Seniors

Margaret M. Mead

Nicole,
For my future roommate!
♡ Sarah
xx

Golden Years Lifestyle

ISBN: 978-1-64999-752-4 (Print)
ISBN: 978-1-64999-755-5 (Ebook)

Golden Years Lifestyle

Mission Statement

To build supportive, safe environments for people to grow into their golden years with dignity. To bring together like-minded 55+ people to live together. To build a community of lifelong friendships. To provide an opportunity for investment and ownership in a property. To enjoy independence. To share day to day laughter and challenges. Trust is the foundation for all that we do. Helping young-minded 55+ people enjoy each day as they continue their exciting new life while living together yet maintaining their independence. ***We believe that living in harmony and being supported by our friends leads to a longer, healthier, happier life***

Dedication

For my father, my greatest teacher, who taught me,

"Our word is our bond, make sure it is a good one. It is the only thing people will remember us by."

- *Cedric Alan Sykes Greenhill D.F.C., F.R.I.*

Table of Contents

Foreword

I was introduced to Margaret in June of 2019 by my business partner. When I first met her, she had this amazing idea that I had not heard before.

As a business consultant, I talk to and work with a lot of business owners with great businesses. However, what struck me about Margaret's idea was that it was unique and well-timed for the current market. I was familiar with the studies done about baby-boomer populations in North America and the coming of the greatest wealth transfer in modern history. But I had not thought of the individual needs of baby-boomers as they retire but still want their independence and freedom of movement.

And this is where Margaret had hit the nail on the head. I remember that June day, I could see the potential of her idea, which was barely in its formulation stage and I knew immediately that I wanted to participate and contribute to her endeavour.

Fast forward 1 year later, and here we are. The idea has now blossomed into a 100-year vision and is a legacy project that will benefit future generations. I am so proud of Margaret and how far she has come starting with a simple one-house idea that now will take off in a big way.

I look forward to what comes next for *Golden Years Lifestyle* and its owner Margaret M. Mead.

Iffy Kazim
Operations
Business Training Pro

July 1, 2020

Acknowledgments

Thank you my two beautiful daughters Victoria and Diana. You have always encouraged me to follow my dreams. Writing this book and creating *Golden Years Lifestyle* is a dream come true. My sister Janice, you are my biggest cheerleader and fan. I am blessed to have a family who over the years have listened to my wild ideas and still look forward to hearing more. Nancy, twenty years ago sitting at your kitchen table talking about something like this, now *Golden Years Lifestyle* has come to life. Tina, I cherish your friendship. Thank you for your time and effort you gave me with completing this book. Alex, thank you for designing my website. It is wonderful. Andrew and Ruth, thank you for your support and wisdom. My very good friends who love me and believe in me. Thank you from the bottom of my heart, you know who you are. A big thank you to my team without whom this project would not have taken off.

Iffy, you are my rock.

A special thank you to Julia, you set me up and really got me going.

For all this, I am truly grateful.

Who is Golden Years Lifestyle?

Vision

Golden Years Lifestyle is a corporation that is dedicated to building new homes or obtaining existing homes with the intention of retrofitting them to accommodate seniors' needs as we grow older.

Mission

We bring together like-minded 55+ people who each buy a percentage of the home, maintaining ownership while living in the home.

Values

Harmony - We believe that housemates should be able to live in peace with their environment and with confidence.

Friendship - Create an environment where people can share their past experiences and create new ones.

Security - Security in knowing that they have someone there.

Togetherness - Co-owners become comfortable with their chosen family building trust and happiness.

Reliability - *Golden Years Lifestyle* is always there for you as one of the co-owners to support the management of the property. Your ideas are our inspiration.

Stability - *Golden Years Lifestyle* creates forever-homes that addresses all the needs of people going into the next chapter of life.

A Good Question To Ask

"Is this book for me?"

This book IS for you!

If you are open to the possibility of co-owning a home with 3-4 other like-minded people.

If you are someone who is at the point in life when you are wondering what alternatives you have other than moving into a senior's residence or with your grown children and their family.

If you are married and your family has left the nest, and your home is taking more time to look after than you would like.

If you like the company of others.

Imagine living in a home where...

People are sitting together, playing games, discussing what they will have for dinner, enjoying a glass of wine by the fireplace, sharing past experiences and laughing through the new ones.

A new chosen family has been created. Each person has a sense of belonging and they are not alone. They are enjoying their golden years.

Companionship is the cornerstone of *Golden Years Lifestyle*. People feel like they are appreciated and loved. They know that they have fellow housemates that are on the same journey as they are. They feel comfortable, at ease and at peace with their new family members.

They are participating in various activities such as gardening and growing vegetables.

There is a sense of harmony in the home environment. The living space is warm, inviting, happy, and healthy. There is a sense of ease and togetherness.

It is an active home, where friends and family congregate together. This home is alive.

It's a whole world within itself. We look forward to creating more happy memories and living with purpose. Our desire in life is not just existing, **it's living**.

Never doubt that a small group of thoughtful, committed citizens can change the world; indeed, it's the only thing that ever has."

Margaret Mead, Anthropologist

Chapter One

Why I have decided to choose this lifestyle.

The importance of togetherness was instilled in me at an early age. My younger years were spent living amongst many girls in boarding schools. I found myself enjoying the atmosphere of living with my peers and participating in activities that were of common interest. Of course, there were differences. However, we had the freedom to spend on our own to pursue personal interests. Thinking back to my boarding school days, I often think to myself, "*How perfect that set up was!*" I was able to maintain my independence, however, if I had a bad day, there was someone there for me to talk to about it. These formative years have left a deep imprint on me.

Here I am in my sixties. Where did the time go? It feels like yesterday when getting together with my girlfriends for fun, we would talk about our plans for our "old age." What does that really mean? "Old Age?" For me, it is my "Golden Age." I feel grateful that my health is good as this has me feeling wealthy beyond words. I enjoy writing books and walking my dog any time of day or evening. I have two wonderful daughters, a large happy extended family, and genuine friends who absolutely love me for who I am.

Being an independent person, asking for help when I need it, and getting along fine without it is natural for me. My life is brilliant, and I am grateful for every aspect of it. However, there are just some days when I simply feel lonely. Sometimes after a long day of running around showing properties, I would love to walk in my door to an already cooked meal and hearing someone asking me how my day went. For years I've had a dream of living with a group of people who are like minded, who respect one another who loves to be close to the land, and who love life.

Living alone when there is a scare like a pandemic bringing with it a life of temporary isolation is scary. Creating a safe place for people to live together in a community is what *Golden Years Lifestyle* is offering. A willingness to continue living a life of being who we are while living in a home with a few other people is comforting. These homes are here for people to come together to form a bond of lifetime friendships.

Whether you are married and live in a home with other married couples, or with single people, it really does not matter. Any combination of people in the home will be determined by choice. Many seniors are married; however, as they age their house begins to feel too large. Yet they still want to live in a home rather than a residence with hundreds of others.

One of the spouses may worry that in the event of their death, they'd leave their loved one behind to fend for their future all alone. Imagine living in a shared home creating a new family, and when one spouse departs, the rest of the new family gathers to offer support and love. Best of all, there is no upheaval, as all the major decisions have been made years in advance.

I believe I am fulfilling my purpose by helping young minded 55+ people come together to live the rest of their lives in harmony and love. I am helping as many people as possible to live their lives with a sense of self-worth and fulfillment. Their viewpoint counts, and they deserve to choose the way they live their lives. Sometimes when we are on our own, whether it is in a house or apartment by ourselves or in a retirement home or long term care facility, being alone is what is in our mind much of the time. Personally, I enjoy being around people. I love interacting with people, learning new things, and sharing what I have learned. For these reasons, I believe that co-living is a lifestyle I want to enjoy.

Does any of this resonate with you? Are you a person that enjoys being independent? Who do you know who is currently living alone and who is lonely or is depressed? Have you ever thought you are ready for something new?

Golden Years Lifestyle creates alternatives for people at a time in their life when the question comes up, "What's Next?"

As society reaches a point where we as baby boomers are in the next chapter of our lives if you aren't living alone now, is there a chance you may be soon? If you are living on your own, do you think it may be time for a change? My desire to bring people together, both men and women, to co-exist and to live a life of learning and sharing is my passion.

Loneliness is everywhere. I refer to the loneliness one feels after our family has moved on. Sometimes after being out all day, knowing I am going to be by myself when I get home, I have feelings of loneliness, which is different from being alone. Memories of the hustle and bustle of a home with movement, laughter, and shouts of joy come to my mind. My thoughts go to memories of a life with my children and how we had a good-night ritual of "always clearing the air before we went to sleep." I used to tell my children, "we go to sleep happy, and we wake up happy." Whatever happened that day, I believed we could sort it out before we went to sleep. I made sure the last words the girls heard at night were, "I love you."

Imagine hearing the words "I love you" before you went to bed. It may not be every day you hear these words as we did. However, can you imagine saying these words and then hearing them repeated back to you? Love is the greatest gift anyone can offer and imagine how wonderful it would be to give and receive these words for the rest of our lives.

As you age, would it be safe to say that health is your number one concern? We don't know how long our bodies will continue functioning healthily. Some of us have had family and friends who one day was healthy, then in a flash, or what seemed like a flash, their health deteriorated, and they were forced to leave their homes. Moving was left up to their immediate family, usually their grown children. This was and is, for most people, a traumatic situation. *Golden Years Lifestyle* can help you make the best choice for your future so you may enjoy living a long and healthy life surrounded by friends who love and appreciate you. Most of all, we offer the possibility of *never having to move again!* Now, can you imagine that?

"Aging is not 'lost youth' but a new stage of opportunity and strength."

Betty Friedman

Chapter Two

The 80/20 Rule

When my children ask me, "mum, how are you?" and they hear, "I'm great!" They believe me 80% of the time. When I say this, I am not saying that they feel I am lying 20% of the time; it is normal for grown children of ageing parents to worry. I am happy and healthy; I am lucky to be able to say this.

However, on occasion, when walking my dog, I have tripped and fallen. Once, I had my daughter on the phone and somehow missed a crack in the sidewalk. My boot caught the uneven cement and poof, I was down hard. I bruised my knee and banged my face and elbow. I was so surprised all I could do was lie there until I caught my breath. My daughter was frightened and very concerned and was ready to call an ambulance. Luckily, some people saw me fall and, within a few seconds, were right by me offering their help. Once I was on my feet, I reassured my daughter I was fine.

That fall was over six months ago now. As I age, I notice my body (as happy as it is) when hurt, doesn't bounce back as quickly as it once did. To this day and most likely every day moving forward when my daughter asks me, "mum, how are you?" and I tell her, "I am great," there will be that 20% concern she reserves as she is well aware I am not quite as nimble as I once was.

At the printing of this book I am in my mid sixties...still young in my opinion. As each year comes and goes, I am more and more aware of small things that reflect that I am ageing. One day I will not be able to convince my daughter that everything is "great." There will come a time when instead of my daughter wondering if I am truly telling her the full truth 80% of the time, this will start being 75%, then 70%, and so on. As a co-owner I am sure that my family won't be as concerned knowing that I have others looking out for me. Friends take care of each other.

"We don't stop playing because we grow old. We grow old because we stop playing."

George Bernard Shaw

Chapter Three

Home Alone

Living at home alone while we are in good health is fine. For myself, enjoying the peace and quiet is perfect. At this new chapter of life, people find themselves considering whether or not they should leave their homes. In some extreme cases, financial limitations are why they have to come up with an answer. So many times, I have helped my clients get their homes ready for sale. Often they made this decision to mitigate future financial hardship and loneliness.

As I think about all the people who were stuck at home on their own during the time of self-isolation, I wonder how they coped. So much was broadcast on TV, the news, stories about lonely people who were anxious and sad. I am disheartened to think that their greatest companion was their television. It is no wonder many people suffer from anxiety, depression, and sadness. We are inundated with too much information. When we are on our own, there are times we possibly think too much. Perhaps we make things up and overdramatize the stories we tell ourselves. This isn't the best thing to do, especially if we are trying to remain calm and sane. I wonder how many stories we hear are exaggerated so much that the intention is to upset people. When I think about people with so much time and very little to do, I feel concerned. I want to help. I want to create another way for all of us who are alone, to live happily together.

From the website of Jo Cox, the former British Member of Parliament. Jo Cox was responsible for bringing in a Minster of Loneliness into the United Kingdom.

2018: A minister and government strategy emerge

"I will not live in a country where thousands of people are living lonely lives forgotten by the rest of us." Jo Cox

The Jo Cox Commission on Loneliness is an organization set up following the murder of the British Member of Parliament Jo Cox which planned to find ways to reduce loneliness in the United Kingdom.

At the beginning of 2018, former Prime Minister Theresa May accepted the report's recommendations, kicking off the government's new commitment with a reception to honour Jo Cox and her historic work.

"I am pleased that the government can build on her legacy with a ministerial lead for loneliness who will work with the commission, businesses and charities to shine a light on the issue and pull together all strands of government to create the first-ever strategy," said May at the event.

From there, the country's Minister for Sport and Civil Society added Loneliness to its portfolio, making lawmaker Tracey Crouch the nation's first Minister for Sport, Civil Society and Loneliness. Her assignment: lead a cross-government group to act against loneliness and make the issue a consistent parliamentary priority.

'Minister for Loneliness' Tracey Crouch said: "Nobody should feel alone or be left with no one

to turn to. Loneliness is a serious issue that affects people of all ages and backgrounds, and it is right that we tackle it head-on." Oct 15, 2018

Kathy Lee Gifford, former host of the *Today* show, talks about her experience with loneliness and its crippling effects.

The following information is taken directly from MARKET WATCH Published: Jan. 28, 2020 at 10:21 a.m. ET'

By Catey Hill

"From the outside, the former "Today" show host — she left the long-running NBC CMCSA, +0.84% morning program in 2019 — seemed to be living a life that many would covet, including a successful career and two children who'd recently gotten engaged. But in recent years, she's endured her share of losses: Her husband, the former NFL halfback and sportscaster Frank Gifford, died in 2015 in their home in Connecticut; her mom died, and her adult children had left home.

That empty house "came to feel like a mortuary with me just there alone," Gifford told the "Today" show this week. "The loneliness was crippling." So, she recently moved to Franklin, Tenn. — a city about 20 miles south of Nashville.

"I moved here because I was dying of loneliness," Gifford told the Tennessean in an interview. "Here's the bad news — I'm a widow, an orphan and an empty nester. The good news is, I have the freedom of a widow, an orphan and an empty nester. I've got all the time to spend my days writing. I'm having the life I could've only ever dreamed of."

She's not alone in loneliness. One in three older adults feels lonely, according to a survey released this year of 2,000 adults aged 50 to 80 by the University of Michigan. Specifically, 34% said they felt a lack of companionship (26% sometimes and 8% often), and 27% said they felt isolated from others (22% sometimes and 5% often).

For older adults, a number of factors contribute to these high rates of loneliness: "Their loved ones may no longer be with them. Some may move, some may pass. What's more, ways they interacted with others (work, parents of their children's friends) may not be a part of their life anymore," says psychologist Elizabeth Lombardo, author of "Better Than Perfect: 7 Strategies to

Crush Your Inner Critic and Create a Life You Love."

And for some people, a move may be just what the doctor ordered. Indeed, experts say a move can help curb loneliness – if done right."

People of any social or economic level are prone to loneliness. Kathy Lee Gifford is one of many celebrities who suffer from this immense deep feeling. We often imagine that because celebrities live a busy life and have dozens of people around them, loneliness wouldn't be an issue. Loneliness knows no boundaries.

"Age is an issue of mind over matter. If you don't mind, it doesn't matter."

Mark Twain

Chapter Four

Safety Factors to consider

One of my good friends, Tee, lived on her own after her children left the nest. She lived in a condominium, and she thrived in her independence. Her son and daughter are both married now with children of their own. Although they visited her often, there was a deep feeling she carried with her that they didn't visit enough. They did their best; however, they were busy with their lives, and Tee would sometimes fall into a depression.

She was alone, and although she spent a lot of her time working at home, organizing charity events, and visiting with friends, she would still say living alone was hard for her. Interestingly, her friends saw her as very active; she was always busy. We often talked about living together on a farm, building a few residences so that we could be together yet still have our independence.

Then things started to happen to Tee. She was walking to a store, and as she stepped up onto the sidewalk, she tripped and fell. She broke her arm and badly bruised her legs. Then shortly after this happened, she slipped and fell and broke her hip. This time she was at home, and she couldn't get up nor could she reach the phone. She lay on the floor for hours until luckily one of her neighbours came to check up on her because she wasn't answering her phone and her neighbour knew she was home. The neighbour helped Tee get an ambulance.

What if her door had been locked, and the person gave up and walked away? What if she had been more seriously hurt, and the need for her to get care had been more urgent? What if no one had noticed Tee's absence? With injuries, especially in older age, time can be crucial.

Now, I can assume that as you read that above story, you either thought of a similar story from your own experience or one that you have heard about happening to someone you know. That's because this is constantly happening! Because many individuals are trying to stay on their own, in their homes longer these days, it seems that more cases of injuries occur when people are alone.

I recently received a message from my girlfriend, Mary, telling me her father was outside his home when a couple of people attacked him and took his money. He was slightly hurt: his ego was shaken. He was lucky. It turned out the people were from the neighbourhood and had been watching him for some time. Once they learned his routine, they knew when he would have some money on him. Occurrences like this happen more than we know. Older people living on their own, being watched, and then attacked. I mention this not to scare you; it is a fact. When we grow older, some things change, like our ability to defend ourselves. If more seniors lived in a home shared with friends, the likelihood of someone attacking them as they walk home is less likely. Strength in numbers is the key to safety.

Another close friend of mine, Lilias, has been living alone in her home for 15- years. She has four grown children, a handful of grandchildren, and great-grandchildren as well! Her life is full-- "never a dull moment" as she puts it.

One day Lilias tripped and fell in her garden, breaking both of her arms. When this happened, she could not do anything—not even pick up a cup of tea. Each of her friends took turns staying with her to help with tasks such as cleaning, grocery shopping, and cooking. Lilias was fortunate with having a large circle of friends as it was a few weeks before Lilias felt confident she could be on her own for a few days at a time.

Must we worry about the upkeep of our home?

Where are you living now? Are you in a house, a bungalow, or two-story? Do you live in an apartment or a condominium? It doesn't really matter where you live; if you are on your own, the chances are you are responsible for maintaining your home. There is the cleaning, the upkeep, and the paying of bills. You make sure the garbage is put out on time, the grass is cut, the weeds are pulled, and the snow is shovelled in the winter. You get my drift. Looking after your home is a lot of work. There is a lot to think about. When does it become more difficult to maintain your day to day routines? I think each person has a unique answer.

The idea behind living in a luxurious forever home with three other people, is a shared workload. No longer do you solely have to think about everything that has to be done to maintain your home. It also becomes less expensive to hire outside help. A typical day or week might look like this; Monday morning garbage must be put out. This can be done by one person each week if they so choose, or it can be divided up between the four residents, or lastly, for a fee described below, the *Golden Years Lifestyle Corporation* could handle this chore along with others. One day maybe a grocery shopping day. You would all get together to plan out what the menu will be for the week. Or perhaps you will plan for an evening BBQ in the back yard and you end up inviting some friends to join you. As you live together, you will soon fall into a routine that will suit all of you.

Outdoor maintenance is a task where *Golden Years Lifestyle* offers assistance. Adding garbage removal is a simple step based on the desire of the residents. *Golden Years Lifestyle* offers a checklist of all the components of living in a home and the running of it. *Golden Years Lifestyle* is here to assist in every capacity as needed.

A group of four friends recently bought a home and are now living together. They call themselves The Golden Girls. Over the years they worked out a plan for the day to day chores and how they look after everything. In their situation, they do not have a corporation like *Golden Years Lifestyle* to oversee the running of the home. They have chosen to make all the decisions. In our home, *Golden Years Lifestyle* will manage to look after the major things that must be done. Our intention is for the residents to enjoy living in their homes. No one needs to worry about who is going to shovel the snow.

Do you want your family to become 24/7 caregivers?

Of course, we don't! I have not met one person living on their own who would relish the thought of having one or many of their family look after them in their home. Most seniors are young minded people who are fiercely independent. Living on our own is what we want to do. This is great for as long as it lasts. When does it become apparent that our independence is starting to disappear? Did it happen gradually or perhaps suddenly? In either case, you are living on your own. For a while, it was a great experience. However, we are talking about when the day comes when we really need help.

When we are working, we maintain our regular routine. We have a purpose—a beginning and end of our day. We spend our days in communication with people outside of our home. Even if we come home to an empty house, our days are filled with drive and socialization to help fulfill us.

However, once we finish working, typically around the age of 65, many of us new retirees struggle to find a new sense of purpose. This often leads to more sitting around the house in solitude, feeling lost and isolated. Your children may notice that you aren't getting out as much and feel obligated to check up on you more often. As we get older and live on our own, we tend not to want to cook as regularly as we once did.

At our local seniors' centers, they usually dedicate one or two days a week where lunch is served at a very reasonable price. These days the center is packed. If we don't cook for ourselves regularly or attend a center and enjoy a decent lunch, our health tends to deteriorate. This means more health appointments that our grown children need to take us to. Once again, pulling them away from their lives to help us with ours. As our abilities weaken, we also find ourselves asking for help more often. If we used to be able to hang our Christmas lights on our own, perhaps now we need to call our son or granddaughter to do it for us. *Every call you need to make for help causes you to feel more alone.* Our need to have the connection of someone around us is strong.

Celia's Story

My own sister used to tell me, "they'll have to carry me out of my house feet first," and although she died in a hospital, she was one of the lucky ones as she was able to live in her home until the very end. When her husband died, she was left alone in her home, however not for long. In no time flat, her grandson, Kevin, moved in to keep her company. He let go of his apartment, changed his job, and happily moved in. The two of them loved living together with their many cats. I think they had four of them at this point.

Then, a few years later Kevin's mother, my sister's middle daughter, became single again. After selling her own house she chose to move back home with her mother. This worked out well as Kevin was ready to move on from his grandmother. Over the years, my sister's house became a safe and wonderful place for people to come and go constantly.

Towards the end of her life, her son, David, moved into her home as well and became her primary caregiver as she was diagnosed with cancer. He gave up his life in L.A. left everything behind temporarily to be with his mother until the very end. Between his sisters and him, they drove her to treatments at the hospital, and to doctor's appointments. David stayed with her at home, giving his sisters the freedom to visit their cottages occasionally during the summer. My sister was very fortunate, as she never felt alone. As I said, she was definitely one of the lucky ones. We are not all that fortunate to have children or family drop everything to look after us.

Cognition is "the mental action or process of acquiring knowledge and understanding through thought, experience, and the senses".

Wikipedia

Chapter Five

Retirement Homes

You could sell your home and move into a nursing home or a residence with all the bells and whistles. Your family may help you to set this up and with the equity generated from your home, you can happily live on this income until it runs out. We are living longer statistically. This scenario of selling your home then moving into a luxury residence comes with a downside as well as the initial upside. Mainly running out of money and then being faced with having to move into another dwelling, perhaps not such a luxurious residence as the one you are forced to leave.

The following information is directly from the website. ***https://www.betterseniorscare.ca/***

There is no better way to express where we are and what our options are.

"The facts about long-term care are clear. More than 90% of Ontario Seniors living in long term care suffer from cognitive impairment. 50% of Ontario's long-term care homes need to be rebuilt. More than one million care hours are taken away from our seniors each year and spent on government paperwork."

"Ontario health policy seems to have largely forgotten that seniors' needs matter. ... Thank you to the over 80,000 Ontarians who helped us make change happen by ... Together we can empower policy changes to improve the lives of seniors ... of residents by rebuilding today's homes and increasing capacity for tomorrow."

The following information is taken directly from the website: *www.oltca.com/oltca*

'About long-term care in Ontario: Facts and figures.'

"In the past five years, the long-term care sector has undergone profound change. Before then, long-term care homes accommodated a mix of

residents with low to very high care needs. Since 2010 however, only people with high or very high care needs are eligible for long-term care in Ontario. These changes are largely due to the province's ageing-in-place strategy, which has made more funding available for care at home while implementing new, stricter admission criteria for those entering long-term care. The result: Ontario seniors are entering long-term care homes when they are older, frailer, and in need of more medical and personal care than ever before."

"Our seniors need long-term care homes that are ready and capable of meeting their ever-increasing, complex health care needs and able to provide safe quality care when they expect and require it most. Visit us at betterseniorscare.ca to learn more about how the government and homes can work together to build the capacity for care. And below, you can find some quick facts about residents, long-term care homes, costs and eligibility."

Costs

Looking at government-sponsored Long Term Care Homes in Ontario, here are some examples of costs you can expect in 2021. This is an average, and it is up to each person to do his or her own research. These amounts are examples only.

Private Room: $2,701.61 / month

Semi-Private Room: $2,280.04 / month

Basic Room: $1,891.31 / month

The truth is I can go on. My suggestion is for you to go online and do your own research. However, I offer you another option as to where you may live in the future. I am determined to set myself up so that if or when my circumstances change, I am already in a home with my housemates for life. Here is Lucy's story as she is living it today.

Lucy's story

Lucy is an only child. When her parents lived in their three-story townhome, they were happy, and they enjoyed many years in their home. Her mother busily enjoyed shopping, and the shops she enjoyed frequenting were within walking distance from her home. Her father never quite retired as he consistently consulted in the business he had worked in for over 45 years.

Then things started to change; Shortly after his 80th birthday, he suffered a stroke. Luckily, he partially recovered; however, over time, it became clear that Lucy's mother was overwhelmed with taking care of her home in addition to her husband. Lucy found herself visiting her parents more and more often to check in and help as much as she could.

Eventually, Lucy's father was no longer able to drive, and as her mother never drove, Lucy became their primary source of transportation. Lucy, who herself suffers from chronic pain, found herself needing to help her parents so often that she was no longer able to care for herself. She found herself having to skip her own medical appointments to drive her parents to theirs.

As her father's health began to deteriorate even further, her concern turned into constant worry. and her mental health became affected, as well as her physical health. Lucy became bound to her parents' every need, and she felt that she had no option but to put her own health aside to help her parents.

After a few years, Lucy convinced her parents to sell their home and move into a luxury seniors' residence in Toronto across from a popular mall. This way, her parents could still do what they enjoyed together, walking across the street to do some shopping or visiting a mall cafe.

Within the first year, it became evident that Lucy's father was now afflicted with Alzheimer's, and he started wandering and getting lost in the mall. As this continued, a decision had to be made for her parents to move floors to a more secure unit so that her father wouldn't get lost. I would like to add some prices at this point in Lucy's story. These prices are provided by her directly.

When her parents first moved into the residence, they had a two-bedroom apartment with a kitchenette. They paid $6,600 a month, a rate which included all their meals and snacks, their laundry service, all activities within the home, and some excursions. When they had to move to the secured floor, they were offered a one-bedroom with no kitchenette, and now they were paying $8,800 a month. It then became evident that her mother was starting to show signs of early dementia. The price went up to around $10,000 even though all her parents did was sit in their room, leaving only when escorted to the dining room for a meal. The reason for the price increase was the level of care according to the set guidelines for each level of increased care. The price rose $1,000 for each parent each level. By year three, after moving into the residence, they were paying over $14,000 monthly. Quite a jump!

At this time Lucy decided to move her parents into a nursing home so that they would have enough money to last them until they died. Their financial advisor said they would most likely run out of money before they died based on the rate they were paying out each month. Lucy had already been told by the residence manager that once the money ran out, they automatically moved the residents into a nursing home. The writing was on the wall.

When Lucy made her inquiries as to where she would place her parents, she was restricted to a geographical area as she wanted to be able to visit her parents on a continual basis as this was what she had been doing for several years. She was lucky! Her father was accepted at Lucy's first choice of homes that she had inspected. However, there was a catch; they could only take her father as they did not have a double room. They also did not have two single rooms. Lucy was assured that once her father was living there that her mother would be put at the top of the waiting list. This is what Lucy did.

She placed her father in a single room paying a little under $3,000 monthly. Her mother stayed behind at the residence and had to be told that her husband was at the doctors and that he would be back soon. Fast forward to four months after Lucy's father moved out. Her mother was still alone, and the monthly amount for her apartment was $10,000.

Finally, the call came in. A room became available, and Lucy was able to move her mother into the same nursing home as her father. She was placed on a different floor, as that is all that was available. Lucy hired a caregiver to come to the home to help both her parents with feeding them, making sure they were happy and seeing each other daily. The caregiver that Lucy hired knew her parent's routine, and they knew her. This was an absolute gift because it meant Lucy could loosen up on her visiting times and concentrate on getting the physiotherapy she so desperately needed.

Since they moved into the home, they have been placed on the same floor in their own rooms as a double room was still not available. The cost for both is under $6,000.00 monthly—a far cry from the first residence. Even factoring in the extra help, it is much less. The strain and worry that Lucy carried wondering if her parents would be able to live a good life are now over; however, she is still worried because of the world's current events.

This is Lucy's story in her own words:

"After having made the decision that I needed to move my parents to a long-term care home, I knew that there would be more issues to deal with. When you apply to long term care homes for two parents, it's virtually impossible to get them into the home at the same time. In my situation, a bed for my dad came up first, so I moved him to the home. If one spouse is admitted, the other spouse goes to the top of the waitlist under Spousal Reunification. It still took four months for my mom to get a bed. My parents have always been extraordinarily close. So, separating them was extremely difficult. This situation was stressful for me also. I had to split time between two places, but the worst was knowing how much they missed each other. They have been married sixty-one years. Now that we are going through the COVID19 pandemic, I am alone in my home and unable to visit them. I miss seeing them."

Note: June 2020 Lucy's mother died. Her mother died alone. Lucy was robbed of being able to be with her mother as she was dying and she was not able to say goodbye. In August 2020 Lucy was granted permission to visit her father. For an indoor vist Lucy has to take the COVID test every fourteen days. Even with passing the COVID test Lucy has to wear a mask as well as she is not permitted to hold her fathers hand as she has to stay six feet away from him. Her father is hard of hearing as well as he is suffering from advanced dementia and Lucy doesn't know if her father knows it is her. In the past she would hold his hand and he would give it a squeeze.

Ann's Story

Ann's mom was in a long term care home for approximately three years. March 12th. 2020 was the last time she was to see her mother because of the Covid-19. She would call the home every day to check on her but felt her mom was slipping away each and every day. Her conversation would start with her mom asking "when are you coming to see me", and as always Ann assured her she would come that day. In Ann's own words, "the most awful feeling was losing my mother on June 12th. 2020 and not being allowed to see her or talk to her in person. My mom had apparently fallen two times and I knew her heart was giving out however I didn't want to believe she was dying. The night before she died they reassured me that she was fine and the Dr. assured me she was okay. Losing my mother this way is no way any human should be treated. My heart is so heavy with sadness. The last words I heard from the PSW was that your mom did not die of Covid-19 but the absence of not seeing you was a factor".

"If there is one thing I've learned in my years on this planet, it's that the happiest and most fulfilled people are those who devoted themselves to something bigger and more profound than merely their own self-interest."

John Glenn

Chapter Six

Why Would a 55+ Young Minded Person Choose to Co-own?

The number of Canadians who are seniors and are going to be in their seventies or older in the next decade is close to ten million people across Canada. Where are they living now and where will they be living out their golden years? I have discussed the seniors' homes and luxury residences as far as the cost; however, I feel another area is more important. This concern relates to giving up the freedom to make choices such as when you want to eat your meals, what you want to eat, and having the ability to participate in preparing the meals. Most importantly, when the meal is cooked, enjoy it while it is still hot.

What is forgotten when living in an institutionalized establishment is the fun of something as simple as setting the table together as a group or with one member of the household. Washing the dishes and tidying up after the meal is fun because it becomes a time to chat about anything. Joy arises from being together as a close-knit group and sharing different activities. Going out shopping for the food or choosing to have it delivered from the supermarket means you get to make the decision. Sharing a home together means you can watch TV and enjoy choosing the shows you want to watch and at what time.

There is something to be said about living among a few selected people in a house rather than in an establishment where an employee makes most decisions. The needs of the many outweigh the needs of a few. The activity time schedules, the mealtimes, and the menu planning, all must be thought out and scheduled well in advance. The cost of the food or the percentage of the food waste must be factored in, and this price is reflected when the amount paid by the individual is worked out. The activities are planned according to the needs of the majority in the home. There is not as much flexibility as there would be in a private home. How could there be?

Living in a privately owned home, knowing your name is on the title, and having the freedom to make choices is more rewarding than being looked after in a residence. The experiences are quite different. One is not better than the other.. A privately-owned home with fewer people is quieter. Also if you are worried about what will happen to your spouse, this is a great option to make sure they will be looked after and not alone. Knowing everyone intimately is more comforting for most of us.

Another consideration as we age is how we feel about ourselves when we no longer have a purpose in life. Many older people I speak to live day to day, not really doing very much. Yes, they may go out occasionally; they may visit the seniors' center and enjoy the company of their peers. They may get together with their family. However, many admit they suffer regularly from boredom. If they live alone, sometimes they lose their motivation to experience new things. Simple things like cooking themselves a tasty meal becomes more of a rarity rather than a normal daily habit.

When we live on our own, in our own home, how often do we have friends or family over for a meal? How many times do we invite a friend over to watch a show or to play a game of cards? Looking into the future and looking at what other people experience living together, will in the long run bring out the best of us.

If you currently own your home and wonder where to invest your money once you have sold, a *Golden Years Lifestyle* home is an option. **Reinvest in yourself**. Own your shared home!

Some interesting information: taken from the website. ***www.150.statcan.gc.ca.***

"Starting in 2011, the first year that the baby boom cohorts began turning 65, the increase in the number of seniors in Canada has accelerated. According to preliminary estimates, 17.2% of the country's population were aged 65 and older on July 1, 2018, compared with 14.4% on July 1, 2011. The proportion of seniors is expected to continue to rise rapidly in the coming years as more baby boomers turn 65. According to the most recent demographic projections, one in five Canadians should be aged 65 and older in 2024."

"According to the 2011 Census, 9.6 million Canadians were baby boomers (stats Canada). In 2018, 17.2% of the population was aged 65 years of age or older. Based on Statistics Canada's figures, they predict that 1 in 5 Baby Boomers will be aged 65 or older by 2024. These numbers show that we are currently in a period of rapid growth for baby boomers entering retirement age."

"If there is one thing I've learned in my years on this planet, it's that the happiest and most fulfilled people are those who devoted themselves to something bigger and more profound than merely their own self-interest."

John Glenn

Chapter Seven

Bill 69 2019 Golden Girls Act

"Currently the Planning Act provides that the authority to pass by-laws under certain sections of the Act does not include the authority to pass a by-law that has the effect of distinguishing between persons who are related and persons who are unrelated in respect of the occupancy or use of a building or structure or part thereof, including the occupancy or use as a single housekeeping unit. The Bill amends the Act to provide that the rule applies, for greater certainty, in respect of unrelated seniors."

"All levels of government should recognize that Ontario has an ageing population and should encourage innovative and affordable housing solutions for seniors. Local municipalities should not deter seniors from choosing affordable housing options and should recognize that unrelated seniors living together can reap significant health, economic and social benefits. It is desirable to provide clarity to municipalities that the Planning Act should be interpreted in a way that encourages and permits home sharing by unrelated seniors as a housing solution."

www.ola.org/en/legislative-business/bills/parliament-42/session-1/bill-69

What Co-Owning a Home Looks/Feels Like

Where are you right now with your financial situation? How are you looking after your responsibilities? If you have more money coming in every month to cover your bills and maintain your living, then the question may be, how much money do you have leftover each month? Do you have enough money to go on a holiday, or to buy birthday presents for your friends and family? Even though you may have enough money to exist, do you have enough left over to live happily enjoying knowing you will be well taken care of even when you are too old to pay your bills? Have you thought about a plan to look after yourself over the next twenty or thirty years? Where do you see yourself living? Will you have enough money to perhaps pay someone to live in your home to look after you?

The story below is told from the perspective of Louise, one of the members of 'The Golden Girls' home in Port Perry, Ontario, Canada. She shared with us some of the experiences that living together with her friends has brought her so far. It has been a number of years since they moved in together, and they are doing very well indeed. All four women were single, and all owned their own homes. It was Louise and Bev who first came together with the idea of co-owning a home. They knew a builder who was able to help them design and build their home. They then advertised for two additional housemates to co-own with them. This continues a successful venture for all housemates. Their lives have been filled with many experiences paving the way for future co-owned homes.

We got lucky. Bev and I were the first ones in, and we did a fair bit of "scenario" talk. So, you get up in the morning...then what? How do you see Christmas working? Etc. Martha had been involved in promoting the concept from the outset and we both knew her.

We don't post the house rules. They do change over time. For example, we didn't think about scents. We're now trying to be scent-free. As another example, initially, we agreed that we wouldn't have a TV or music in the living room. That has changed, but we are still very mindful of not putting the TV on if others are around unless there's something we all want to watch. The biggest change was in our shopping. It took some time to evolve the shopping guidelines, but now it's basically, no matter how good the sale is unless YOU are going to use it up, don't buy it! If there are grandchildren in the picture it's important to talk that out and make sure that you all enjoy them. That could be a deal-breaker". Ultimately, you and your housemates set the rules of the home together.

Taken from *https://www.durhamregion.com/*

"The latest guide — one of four released by the province since September — was officially unveiled in Scugog on Dec. 11 when Steve Clark, Ontario's minister of municipal affairs and housing, dropped by to visit the Golden Girls, who now share a renovated heritage home at 100 Perry St. in Port Perry."

"Clark acknowledged that co-ownership of a home — described as a shared living arrangement

where two or more people own and live in a home — is "a fairly new concept" in some communities, but noted that it's growing in popularity in some demographics such as young families looking to enter the housing market or seniors looking to downsize or avoid social isolation."

"Ontario right now doesn't have enough of a mix of housing to meet people's needs at every stage of their life," said Clark.

"As a result," he continued, "the province has developed a series of guides to promote different approaches to homeownership that look at new and innovative ideas to address Ontario's housing crisis."

"The co-ownership guide, available online at www.ontario.ca/housinginnovation, looks at the types of arrangements (individuals or families sharing a home), financing, regulatory requirements and legal issues, as well as upkeep and shared responsibilities."

"Other guides in the series focus on adding a secondary suite, life leases and advice on building or buying a tiny home."

"The guide has all of the answers in it. Municipalities will see very, very clearly this kind

of housing is legal, is allowed ... and it's desirable," said Martha Casson, who shares the Port Perry home with Beverly Brown, Louise Bardswich and Sandy McCully. "We were part of the housing solution — we freed up four homes and nobody had to build them, nobody had to get an incentive or anything."

"The idea of unrelated people keen on equally sharing ownership of a home encountered challenges about five years ago from Scugog council, led by Mayor Chuck Mercier at that time when a local builder approached the township to secure the necessary permits to build a home that wouldn't feature a traditional ownership structure." - Sabrina Byrnes/Torstar

"Across Ontario, there are many empty-nesters who are ready to downsize. They want to but they can not afford to nor can they find a home that suits their need to be close to family or their friends. This is a genuine problem and concern causing a lot of seniors to feel stuck."

"When you get to my age, you'll really measure your success in life by how many of the people you want to have love you actually do love you."

Warren Buffett

Chapter Eight

Picking Housemates, Flexibility is the key

When I think about living with three or four other people, it feels natural. I lived with thirteen people in a home in Victoria BC when I graduated from high school. That was back in the '70s when co-living was commonplace. Many homes housed single young people, as well as couples all living under one roof. I remember it with a great deal of fondness. We never fought, we shared in the preparation of meals, we all helped keep the home tidy and clean.

In this scenario, we had Brian, who we called "the house captain". He was responsible for bringing in any new housemates as well as letting us know the house rules. On many occasions, we enjoyed preparing meals together. As a resident in the home, I was responsible for paying my share of the expenses, and for respecting others' privacy. We all made an effort to remain open-minded so that when any discord did occur, we all sat down and discussed the situation and came to a mutual solution.

Fast forward to today, looking at what would be important for me when choosing a housemate. Characteristics I'd value include respect, honesty, communication, trust, and a willingness to remain open to other people's ideas and opinions. All decisions regarding the home would be agreed upon by all the housemates. In the case of a discrepancy, everyone would have a chance to express their view, and *Golden Years Lifestyle* can be called upon to mediate if needed.

Do you feel it is important to live in a home with housemates who share similar beliefs? Can you see yourself living in a home where your viewpoint in politics or religion is respected? Having shared values is especially important. I cherish how my parents raised me. They instilled the idea that we are all valuable in our own way. To honour thy neighbour as thyself is one of the most important lessons I have learned. Open communication, respect, and the willingness to resolve issues will ensure a warm and caring environment.

How do the housemates choose each other? Word of mouth is a popular way to find someone. In addition, advertising for people of like minds who seek this lifestyle is effective. In this scenario, the first person to commit to a home will be the leading influence in the choosing of the next housemate. An example of setting up a rule or expectation is as follows—if a person is highly sensitive to perfume and they must live in a fragrance-free home she may be clear about her needs. This will be the first item on the guideline list for that home, and the following potential housemates will have to agree to the existing guidelines as they enter the home. Then when we have two people who have committed to the process, they will have the choice to choose the third person. When we have three people, they will choose the fourth.

Each person coming into the home has an opportunity to express what they are unwilling or unable to live with. Everyone has a choice to choose whether this particular home is the one for them. *Golden Years Lifestyle* has contracts for the different scenarios; each home is independent, and the people living in them will reflect this. In the event someone is the second or third person to look at a home and discovers that their needs are quite different, *Golden Years Lifestyle* will look at how to work with this person to locate another home and set it up with their requirements as a top priority and everyone following will agree to this.

To do this requires a process of interviews, asking a lot of questions, and filling in questionnaires. Consider what you would like in a housemate. This knowledge will be an important part of choosing your housemates. Each person will have an opportunity to fill in a questionnaire that includes questions about non-negotiable preferences for you. You'll have a chance to clearly state what you can and cannot live with.

Golden Years Lifestyle will draw on multiple resources to create thorough questionnaires. This is how The Golden Girls in Port Perry came to one of their requirements in their home. When designing the home, they soon discovered they would need two dishwashers in the kitchen because all the women unanimously agreed that leaving dirty dishes in the sink was absolutely not acceptable. Another decision they made after moving in together was to buy only the food needed for that week's menus. When they bought food in large quantities because it was on sale, it resulted in some of the food being thrown out because it wasn't consumed fast enough.

In each home, the homeowners will make up their own lists. However, one rule across all *Golden Years Lifestyle* houses is that smoking is prohibited in the home. The reason for this is first and foremost the safety of the housemates, as well the lingering odour of stale smoke which is neither pleasant nor healthy. We strive to keep the homes clean and odour free.

From here, it will be up to the housemates to choose for themselves what they are comfortable living with. One guideline could pertain to volume. Are you sensitive to loud music? If so, perhaps you are looking for housemates that enjoy listening to their music, or TV at a respectful level—a volume where everyone can still hear each other while talking.

Some people love living in an exceptionally immaculate house and others enjoy a more relaxed approach. Washing floors, walls, windows, vacuuming, cleaning kitchens and bathrooms are tasks not all of us want to do. However, these tasks must be done; so *Golden*

Years Lifestyle will have someone who enjoys cleaning do the cleaning for you.

Another example might be a pet-free home because of allergies. If you are a person who is sensitive to dander you may want a home that is dander free. This isn't really a major requirement as it is more to do with respect for each other's personal needs for their health. On the other hand, if it is a life-threatening situation for someone then of course it will be discussed prior to the signing of any contracts. Each home will determine what factors are considered a priority and non-negotiable.

We, as an aging population, have come to a place in our lives where we have years of living experience behind us. Now, as we create our new life, we always have the opportunity to do our best to openly talk about our feelings in a safe environment. In marriages, we sometimes hide our feelings; with our children, we hide our feelings; with our peers in the workplace, we hide our feelings. In our *Golden Years Lifestyle* homes, we have an opportunity to open up. We can encourage each other to talk about what is in our heads and hearts, or what is in the past that keeps us from living in the present.

I envision harmony in the homes. Yes, it will be a learning experience; it may involve risk. We will strive to trust each other as we talk and to trust that we will be heard. We have that in common, we belong to each other. We trust all is good in our world. Our home is our world. We are here to make this planet with our home on it a better place for all.

As *Golden Years Lifestyle* grows, and the demand increases for these self-sufficient homes, the sky's the limit as to how these co-ownership homes will evolve. This concept isn't a new one. For generations, families have looked after one another, living together under one roof. It is only in the last century our society has become more fractured. Therefore, a commitment from *Golden Years Lifestyle* will be to meet with the housemates on a regular basis to check in to make sure everyone is happy, healthy, and living the life they deserve in their golden years.

"Only by owning who and what you are can you start to step into the fullness of life. Every year should be teaching us something valuable. Whether you get the lesson is really up to you."

Oprah Winfrey

Chapter Nine

Setting Up the House

There are many builders we enjoy working with and when choosing a home, quality comes to mind. Depending on where you may wish to live our builder has several homes to choose from. Imagine living in a unique, elegant luxury home. We are working with a family-owned business for over 30 years, and they are continuously improving their home designs, making them senior friendly.

Golden Years Lifestyle will, with the help of our designers, furnish the main rooms of the homes. Our desire is for the homes to remain timeless, so the homes will be neutral in colour and style of furniture. Comfortable furniture is high on the list. Items such as electric lift chairs may be enjoyed. Our designers will set up the kitchen, dining room, family room, living room, and any other common rooms. The bedrooms and common area in the lower level for the future live-in caregivers will also be set up by *Golden Years Lifestyle*.

As far as your personal space, each bedroom will have an ensuite bathroom and a generously sized closet. Everyone will bring their own bedroom furniture. If you have artwork that you would like to donate to the home, this will be considered. For example, in the Port Perry home, there are a few items that belong to individual women. Their agreement is that while the housemate is alive and living in the home, everyone gets to enjoy it. When she dies, her family will collect the item along with her belongings from her bedroom. The housemates remaining will then look at either replacing the item or not. Each home will be set up to suit the seniors living in it.

In the homes, *Golden Years Lifestyle* is considering three to four garage spaces are available. Depending on how many of the residents still drive, and proximity to stores will contribute to decisions about garage requirements. If you still drive and having your car in the garage is important to you, make sure you are one of the first to register your commitment on a home, as garage parking may be a first-come-first-serve situation. With the Golden Girls in Port Perry, they have an exceptionally long and wide driveway. Thus, two cars parked inside the garage, and the rest stay in the driveway far enough away from the garage so that they can drive around each other's cars so jockeying is not necessary. If *Golden Years Lifestyle* builds a home, then the four residents all may have an indoor parking spot.

When we build a home for the residents, we can design the home according to specific needs. In general, the house will have a porch or a huge deck where the four housemates can all enjoy being together. The bedrooms could have a small sitting room area with a gas fireplace to enjoy in the winter months. When you are ready to make your decision, always remember being the first to register on a home gives you the advantage to contribute your ideas to create the home to your liking. We are creating this home for you and your housemates.

We endeavour to provide the best physical care possible to our housemates. Aside from your own medical doctors, you have access to alternative health care practitioners like Naturopath Doctor, Osteopath, Massage Therapist, Acupuncturist (etc) and supplements that can help us age gracefully. We take your health seriously.

The idea behind each of the homes is to set them up for the next century. After living through COVID-19 and watching the world as it coped with the pandemic, *Golden Years Lifestyle* is more committed than ever to set the homes up so that they are self-sufficient. Therefore, we are looking at growing our own vegetables in a greenhouse, perhaps having solar panels and a well where possible. Having a well-stocked pantry with dried foods and supplies will be essential. In the event of another catastrophe, we want to be well prepared. Self-sufficiency ideas may include dehydrating food, such as meat or fruit, canning vegetables, and having a cold cellar for storing food. These are all things you might enjoy. We will work together to create a healthy environment and have peace of mind knowing the food we eat came from our own kitchen and gardens.

"Some guy said to me, 'Don't you think you are too old to sing Rock n' Roll?' I said, 'You'd better check with Mick Jagger.'"

Cher

Chapter Ten

Financials and Legals

Golden Years Lifestyle will handle the purchase of the homes, all the financials for the running of the homes, some legal costs, as well as the accountant fees related to the home ownership. We can tailor the home ownership equity interest based on your needs and investment. Additionally, we can proactively help to structure the equity interest that suits your individual, and if requested, your unique family situation. As a homeowner, you will be responsible for handling your own personal bank accounts and personal expenses. You will also be engaging your own lawyer to give you independent legal advice and help you navigate through the legal paperwork and legal structure of your invested funds. The taxes and running expenses will vary in each home as each home is independent of one another, and may vary in geographic locations. There is a *Golden Years Lifestyle* management fee that homeowners pay each month. Our contracts outline these figures. Each home will be provided with an outline of all the costs, and each month our bookkeeper will provide a statement for each owner. Management fees will be subject to the cost of living increases.

Ideally, each home is 80% owned by the housemates and 20% owned by *Golden Years Lifestyle*. Depending on the financial situation of each individual person, *Golden Years Lifestyle* may contribute a greater percentage. Our aim is to help as many seniors to own their homes.

Each owner is responsible for asking questions and ensuring they receive all the answers they are looking for. As a household, the housemates are responsible for purchasing groceries and planning their meals. The day to day budget is up to the individual homeowners. We will also encourage homeowners to draft their own individual shared homes rules and guidelines, although *Golden Years Lifestyle* will monitor the co-living space as a neutral service provider. Any additional services may be discussed or requested and the *Golden Years Lifestyle* management will ensure to take it into consideration at the best cost possible.

The homes are non-denominational and politically neutral, which will help minimize confrontations over matters beyond our control. The object of these homes is to provide a safe environment for everyone to enjoy—a place where friends and family get together to celebrate living life to the fullest. *Golden Years Lifestyle* will set up a slush fund for each home so the housemates can celebrate each other's birthdays and other special occasions. Celebrating our golden years together and creating fun filled happy memories is the prime objective of *Golden Years Lifestyle*.

"Aging is an extraordinary process where you become the person you always should have been."

David Bowie

Chapter Eleven

Preparing for Decrepitude

Decrepitude: Noun/ the state of being decrepit.

"He had passed directly from middle age into decrepitude."

Wow, how scary is this? How quickly anyone of us could slide into decrepitude. I am not waiting for this to happen to me. Therefore, I am looking at living in a home with others like myself. No one really knows when we cross over to the other side. In other words, when someone reaches this point, they are worn out and in disrepair. Decrepitude is usually a result of old age or neglect. Elderly people can slide into this state if left alone for too long without enough attention to keep them interested in living. Being of sound mind, happy, and healthy is the opposite of decrepitude. Count me in for this!

Now that I have been on my own for a decade or so, I enjoy reviewing my habits. When do I get up? What is the routine I have created for myself on a day to day basis? How will this change when I am living with three other people? Will I start getting up at a different time? Maybe I will enjoy recreating my day as I will have three other people to think about. What is their daily routine? Do we all want to create new patterns, or will some of us maintain the same schedule that we have gotten used to over the years?

I consider myself to be a flexible person. I can change my mind instantly to accommodate what is taking place in most given situations. If someone has a definite routine I can adjust. For example, if someone must eat at a certain time because of their health, then we as a group will discuss this and come up with a time that is suitable for everyone. Or perhaps I am working, and I may miss the scheduled mealtime, then it might be that my meal is made up and placed in the fridge for me to enjoy when I get home. Or maybe I will miss that meal as I may be eating elsewhere that evening. The meals will be worked out among the group.

We are all individuals leading our own lives while enjoying the companionship of friends when we come home. It could be that a couple of the residents are retired and spend most of their time at home. For them, the structure of mealtimes may be different. They may decide that eating a light breakfast in their room is what they enjoy. We have so many options, each home and the residents in it will create their own schedule. Will there be adjustments to schedules, most likely in the beginning. Monthly meetings come in handy to give everyone the opportunity to talk about what is working and what is not.

I am so excited thinking about living in a home with three or four other people. Whenever I think about what each day may look like, I envision us laughing, talking things out, sharing what our day was like, enjoying a wonderful home-cooked meal together, watching a movie, or playing a game of cards. It really doesn't matter what we do, what's important is the fact that we are not alone and feeling lonely. I do understand that each day may bring different emotions. By all of us being together, we are setting up a support group for ourselves.

There may come a day when we are not able to participate as much as we used to. Our mobility may become more challenged, and we might need a wheelchair, walker or lift. One day we find ourselves having to hire a nurse or a caregiver to assist us with looking after ourselves. When this happens, as a group, we will discuss the logistics and help each other as we age. Coming together now while we are mobile helps us in years to come. Being able to remain in the home as we age into our 90's and beyond is the mission behind *Golden Years Lifestyle* homes. Each home will have at least one bedroom and bathroom along with a sitting room and a small kitchen so that a caregiver may reside in the home.

"There are six myths about old age 1. That it is a disease, a disaster 2. That we are mindless 3. That we are sexless 4. That we are useless 5. That we are powerless 6. That we are all alike."

Maggie Kuhn

Great Idea, But I'm Not Ready Yet

You are more ready than you think.

You may be thinking, "Hey, this is a great idea, but I am not ready yet." For you, we would like to say that is perfectly good. We would like to offer you an idea for your later years when you may be in a state of mind when life starts to change. This option is available to you. When you feel the time has come for you to create your new family, your new community, then *Golden Years Lifestyle* will be here for you.

I invite you to start thinking about decluttering and begin giving your family what you love but no longer need moving forward. A timeline may be one year or perhaps two. It may take *Golden Years Lifestyle* a while to find the perfect location or the perfect housemates for you, so time is on your side. Transitioning yourself into a

Golden Years Lifestyle is a wonderful time. One day this will come to pass.

Think about where you would want to live if you didn't have to move again. How many people would you like to live within the home? If you think co-owning is an interesting idea, then keep it in mind. I encourage you to make the move while you are still young, healthy and wanting more out of life. In the meantime, let me know what you want if this is something you would like to do.

I am an excellent Realtor; I love what I do. In 2021 I will celebrate forty years working full time at this profession. I started working with my father; he was my teacher. He taught me everything he knew. One of the many things he taught me, metaphorically speaking, was to "take your shoes off and put your client's shoes on." I want you to know I will do this with you. I am committed to helping you find the perfect forever golden home so that you too can live out the rest of your days among friends together, all enjoying your *Golden Years Lifestyle.*

Related sites with more information

https://www.ola.org/en/legislative-business/bills/parliament-42/session-1/bill-69

https://oakhillcoliving.wordpress.com/https://www.facebook.com/groups/seniorladieslivingtogether/

https://www.rosehillheights.com/

https://seniorplanet.org/get-involved/online/

https://www.aplaceformom.com/blog/2-27-17-shared-housing-for-seniors/

https://www150.statcan.gc.ca/n1/en/daily-quotidien/190125/dq190125a-eng.pdf?st=N4j3utZa

https://www150.statcan.gc.ca/n1/pub/11-402-x/2011000/chap/seniors-aines/seniors-aines-eng.htm

https://www.marketwatch.com/story/two-years-after-hiring-a-minister-of-loneliness-people-in-the-uk-are-still-lonely-2020-01-29

https://www.canada.ca/en/financial-consumer-agency/services/retirement-planning/cost-seniors-housing.html

https://www.ontario.ca/page/seniors-find-place-to-live

https://www.ontario.ca/page/seniors-find-place-to-live#section-3

https://www.amica.ca

https://www.delmanor.com

https://www.sunriseseniorliving.com

https://www.hqontario.ca/System-Performance/Long-Term-Care-Home-Performance

https://cohousing.ca/about-cohousing/what-is-cohousing/

https://www.ontario.ca/page/housing-innovation

https://www.durhamregion.com/news-story/9778795-port-perry-golden-girls-face-of-ontario-co-ownership-guide/

https://www.oltca.com/oltca/OLTCA/Public/LongTermCare/FactsFigures.aspx

https://goldenyearslifestyle.newulife.com/

Questions and Answers

Are there other cohousing communities?

"In North America, approximately 160 cohousing communities have been completed since 1991 and there are currently more than 100 new communities in various stages of development. The level of social interaction and shared resources varies among communities. A cohousing development seems limited only by the imagination, desire and resources of the group of people who are actively creating their own neighbourhood. Cohousing groups are based on democratic principles that espouse no ideology other than the desire for a more practical and social home environment." Canadian Housing Network

How do I buy into a co-housing arrangement?

Each owner is looking at owning twenty percent (20%) of the house under a tenants-in-common agreement. "The law presumes that a property owned as tenants in common, which means that each owner has a fixed, divided ownership interest, whether it be 20% each or some other combination. On death, each owner's respective interest falls to his or her estate. An owner also can sell his or her share independently of the other owners. *Golden Years Lifestyle* has legal agreements that govern how that will work.

What is the legal agreement about?

Essentially, it covers how one gets in and out of the deal, and how major decisions (e.g., expenditure on a major renovation or repair) will be made, and some general house rules. Either through death or when one owner decides to sell his or her share and move on, it will be important that the remaining housemates like the new buyer. To balance that requirement versus the need to allow someone to get their equity out of the house in a reasonable time frame, there is a 12 month period in which the seller tries to find an acceptable buyer at whatever price the seller can negotiate. If the remaining owners don't accept any of the proposed buyers in that time frame, then they will have two options, buy that share themselves (one or more of the remaining owners) at fair market value, or sell the whole house. The determination of fair market value is spelled out in the agreement.

How will the household be run?

Meals are more fun when shared. We suggest taking turns in planning and cooking a main meal each day. When buying groceries, we suggest an amount be put into the household grocery fund weekly; this will include general groceries, household supplies, and perhaps a bottle of wine to share with others. Any left over money will be diverted to the contingency fund. If you have any special dietary needs, your situation will be discussed with the other housemates, and depending on circumstances you may contribute a different amount than the others to the household grocery fund. Co-owners are responsible for the general upkeep of the home and keeping the common areas clean. *Golden Years Lifestyle* will organize the professional cleaning schedule and manage the cleaning staff once discussed with the house members. Each house member is responsible for the upkeep of their private room.

Who will make the decisions?

Most of the day to day decisions, including menu choices, shopping, food preparation, and similar actions will be made by the owners themselves. Major decisions will be addressed at our *Golden Years Lifestyle* Monthly Meetings. A representative of *Golden Years Lifestyle* will be present at each of these meetings to facilitate and help guide the household to come to a decision. *Golden Years Lifestyle* believes in an effort to practice kindness and a willingness to let things go if they aren't all that important.

Does Golden Years Living have floor plans and who decides on the house decor?

Golden Years Lifestyle works with amazing local designers who will assist in making the common areas of the house such as the kitchen, living room, media room, guest rooms, laundry, and office (if included)warm and inviting. The designers will provide a list of suggested items that everyone will agree upon. Each individual owner will decide how they decorate their bedrooms and bathrooms. As *Golden Years Lifestyle* acquires homes, floor plans, as well as more extensive house details, may be available. Builders and architects will work directly with *Golden Years Lifestyle.*

Is there a monthly fee?

Yes, there is a monthly fee. *Golden Years Lifestyle* will be responsible for paying all the bills relating to the home, Lawyer, Accountant, Management company, and maintaining the property so that the seniors can relax knowing all decisions are taken care of. Legal contracts outline all details of the running of the homes. Monthly meetings with *Golden Years Lifestyle* and the seniors to discuss any changes or improvements are crucial. This is your home, *Golden Years Lifestyle* is here to make the rest of your Golden Years on earth as pleasant, safe, and memorable as possible

What happens if I get sick or I need help?

As you would seek assistance when living on your own, the same would apply here. Your responsibility is looking after your health. Each home provides accommodation for a caregiver if the need arises. Your family is always welcome to help you. The idea is to live independently yet you have the luxury of having housemates who will keep you company while you convalesce.

Is each bedroom equipped with a thermostat that controls the individual heat and air conditioning?

This will depend on each home individually. When a home is built from the ground up, then yes. If it is a home that has been renovated and retrofitted, our builder will address this need, but it may not be a viable option.

What happens when there is a dispute?

Golden Years Lifestyle will conduct monthly meetings with the housemates where issues can be openly discussed. *Golden Years Lifestyle* will mediate when necessary and make every effort to resolve the issue.

What happens if someone dies?

We have legal agreements to cover this question.

Contact *Golden Years Lifestyle* for more information.

Can You Help?

Thank You For Reading My Book!

I really appreciate all of your feedback, and I love hearing what you have to say.

I need your input to make the next version of this book and my future books better.

Please leave me an honest review on Amazon letting me know what you thought of the book.

Thanks so much!

Margaret M. Mead

Made in the USA
Monee, IL
28 May 2023

34862928R00067